Have You Seen the STAR?

Meditation & Poems to Enhance Your Christmas Celebration

JOYCE CARR STEDELBAUER

Look Up!

TATE PUBLISHING, LLC

Published in the United States of America
By TATE PUBLISHING, LLC
All rights reserved.
Do not duplicate without permission.

Appreciation to
International Cooperating Ministries
who published *Have You Met Eve?*
where some of the poems first appeared.

All Scripture references are King James Version,
unless otherwise indicated.

Book Design by TATE PUBLISHING, LLC.

Printed in the United States of America by
TATE PUBLISHING, LLC
127 East Trade Center Terrace
Mustang, OK 73064
(888) 361-9473

Publisher's Cataloging in Publication

Stedelbauer, Joyce Carr

Have You Seen the Star? / Joyce Carr Stedelbauer

Originally published in Mustang,OK:TATE PUBLISHING:2004

1. Christianity   2. Poetry

ISBN 0-9752572-6-9 $14.95

Copyright 2004

First Printing: October 2004

DEDICATION

With love and appreciation

To Dad
our North Star

George
my guiding star

Julie and Dick
Elaine and Mark
our brightest stars

Chelsea, Claire, Ben
Kate and Luke
our rising stars

Scripture quotations used in the book were taken from:

Holy Bible, New International Version ®. Copyright © 1973, 1978, 1984 by International Bible Society. Used by permission of Zondervan Publishing House.

The New American Standard Bible ®. Copyright ©1960, 1962, 1963, 1971, 1972, 1973, 1975, 1977, 1995 by The Lockman Foundation. Used by permission.

The Living Bible. Tyndale House, 1977, ©1971 by Tyndale House Publishers, Inc. Used by permission. All rights reserved.

The Message. Copyright © 1993, 1994, 1995, 1996, 2000, 2001, 2002. Used by permission of NavPress Publishing Group.

ACKNOWLEDGEMENTS

A book of meditation is a window into the soul of the Poet. That window is often clouded and stuck shut. Without the most talented team of Tate Publishing, this window would still be closed. I appreciate and admire:

Rita Tate and her tireless dedication to excellence, both as an editor and mentor,

Kristen Polson for her skill and patience with layout,

Sommer Buss and Anthony Allen for showing the beauty outside the window,

And the entire staff of Tate Publishing who want you to clearly see the Star.

CONTENTS

FOLLOW THE STAR. 11

Eve 20
Tamar 22
Rahab. 24
Ruth 26
David's Mother 28
David 30
Bathsheba 32

Dear Dr. Luke 36
Zacharias. 38
Elizabeth 40
Angel Gabriel 42
Annunciation Day 44

The Innkeeper. 48
The Bethlehem Shepherds 50
King Herod 52

The Wisemen. 56
Simeon 58
Anna. 60

Bethlehem Song 65

REFLECTION 67

*For we have seen His star in the east
and have come to worship Him.*

Matthew 2:2

FOLLOW THE STAR

HAVE YOU SEEN THE STAR? Really seen the Star; the Star of surpassing brilliance, the bright and Morning Star, the Star of hope for a lonely world? Or when you look up is your view of the heavens obscured by trials tall as trees, buildings blocking the blue, polluted air choking out all clarity?

Christmas comes earlier every year—the Poinsettias have barely dropped their leaves when the jingle of faint bells and calendar countdowns arrives.

I love the reality of the Christmas Eve celebration when our family of four generations warms memories by the fire in the light of the bountiful tree. Gifts wrapped with love, food preparations all complete and the children still have the glow of the Christmas candlelight service shining in their eyes.

But between now and then how can I manage not to misplace my joy in the wrappings of gold and silver, cardboard and tape, ribbons and rituals which define everyday life? Whenever I want to meditate on a particular theme I benefit from organizing my thoughts around an acrostic, choosing a particular word for each letter of the word I am considering. So, at the first jingle I remind myself to look up and ask, HAVE YOU SEEN THE STAR? **THE STAR.**

```
Seek
 T
 A
 R
```

There are many worthy words that begin with S—sound, send, secret—but in searching for the Christmas Star I choose SEEK, knowing I must search and research to find out what the Star of the season really means. I know about the Wise Men journeying after a particular new star in the heavens that guided them to Bethlehem. And I ask, why was it so important, and how they knew it was the star of an infant King?

There have been many creditable studies done on the ancient names of the stars found all over the world. The truth of God's story as told in the stars has been corrupted by the Enemy of our souls, obscured in popular occultism so that we are even frightened to look into the Zodiac. We do well to warn of horoscopes and birth charts but we must not disregard what the Holy Scripture reveals so clearly. Indeed the amazing fact is that God has written His story of redemption in the heavens for all earth to see.

The heavens declare the glory of God
Psalm 19
He, who named the stars and set them all in place.
Genesis 1

The ancient names include;
The Branch, He comes, The Prince, The Wounded, The Redeemer, and He shall be exalted.

The Prophet Job knew the heavens well,
God asked him,

Can you hold back the stars? Can you restrain Orion or the Pleiades?
                                                    Job 38

We find the amazing statement,

I, Jesus, have sent my angel to tell you . . . I am both David's root and his descendant. I am the bright Morning Star.
                                                    Revelation 22

Dear Pastor Peter counsels,
We have this word of prophecy made more sure, to which you do well to pay attention, until the morning dawns and the Daystar arises in your hearts.
                                                    I Peter 1.

SEEK the Lord while He may be found.
                                                    Isaiah 55
If you SEEK me you will surely find me.
                                                    Jeremiah 29
SEEK me and live.
                                                    Amos 5

    What incredible promises! Thank you, Lord. But, with every promise there is always a condition, in the same verse, or in the verses preceding or following. So, I make it a practice to mark the promises with a "P" in the margin of my Bible and then a "C" when I find the condition, for until I have been obedient to what God asks I cannot expect the promise to be fulfilled in my life. He says that we must search for Him, be alert to what we see of His handiwork in the universe, concentrate on looking for Him in the Scripture and in believers' lives, if our desire is to find God.

S eek
T rust
A
R

There are many interesting words that begin with T—test, try, tantalizing—but because the Morning Star is Jesus, then I must discover if I can TRUST His words to be true.

So I research David and his grandmother Ruth and the promises of the prophets that Messiah would come to set them free.

I read a Psalm daily and marvel how David the King knew that his only hope of forgiveness was in this magnificent Messiah that was promised to sit on his throne in the future! I, too, kneel in repentance before Him. I form my mouth into praises that elevate my spirit to worship. TRUST grows in my heart as we journey through good times and more stressful times. Year after year we experience God's faithfulness in every situation.

TRUST in the Lord with all thine heart and lean not on your own understanding. In all your ways acknowledge Him and He shall direct your path.
Proverbs 31

In You, O Lord, I put my TRUST.
Psalm 31

David, the poet, expressed his TRUST repeatedly in his songs of praise.

My God, in Him will I TRUST.
Psalm 91

Seek
Trust
Abide
R

There are many compelling words that begin with A—all, always, accept—but I choose, ABIDE. When I SEEK Him to know who He is, The Bright and Morning Star, then I have to choose to TRUST Him, and I know that the very best place for me is to ABIDE in Him.

To dwell in His presence every day of my life.
Psalm 27

He both proceeds and follows me and places His hand of blessing on my head. This is too glorious, too wonderful for me; I can never be lost to His Spirit.
Psalm 139

King David helps me to feel God's Presence. And Jesus gives this clear condition and promise.

If you ABIDE in my Word, then you are truly disciples of mine; and you shall know the truth, and the truth shall set you free.
John 8

Seek
Trust
Abide
Rejoice

There are many wonderful words that begin with R—rest, renewal, reason, but I choose REJOICE! I never liked my name very well, Joyce sounded clipped and uninteresting. I flirted with Constance or Luanne, anything but . . . just Joyce. As I grew up in Faith, I saw the necessity of rejoicing and I hoped it was the root of my name.

David understands well the privilege of rejoicing. His Psalms echo with joy on almost every page.

I will be glad and rejoice in You.
Psalm 9

Rejoice always and again I say rejoice.
Philippians 4

Rejoice, for He is Lord of Lords and King of Kings.
Revelation 17

To praise God during all of the busy days leading up to Christmas is good for my attitude. Whether waiting in long lines, or racing with the clock like the proverbial mouse.

A cheerful heart doeth good like medicine.
Proverbs 17

For who can ever praise Him half enough?
Psalm 145

God inhabits the praises of His people.
Psalm 19

HAVE YOU SEEN THE STAR?

Really seen the Star, the Star of Christmas?

You must SEEK the Star,
You will discover that you can TRUST the Star,
Then choose to ABIDE in the glow of that Star,
And REJOICE in that Star.

There is a blood red cord that twines through Scripture from Genesis to Revelation, from Creation to the Cross to the Tomb and on into Eternity. I invite you to purposely take a little time from your busy days, come sit in your favorite chair with a hot cup of tea and ponder with me the path of the red ribbon that will lead you to see the Christmas Star.

Away in the gray distance of eternity past, God unrolled the first scarlet sunset over the waiting world. The red rays touched all humanity to the end of time.

He set the stars in place and called them all by name.
Genesis 1

He rolled the new moon across the velvet heavens for Signs and seasons.
Genesis 1

For the star of Christmas is none other than The Lord Jesus Christ who declared that one of His beautiful names is The Morning STAR.

When Eve bit the apple,
    Jesus prepared to leave for Bethlehem.

                                      --Jill Briscoe

SEEK...

To SEEK God, or to search for God means to research Him in order to know Him.

> ~ Though He is invisible, He is Omnipresent.
> ~ Though we are limited, He is Omniscient.
> ~ Though we are weak, He is Omnipotent.
> ~ We are fickle, He is Immutable.
> ~ We are angry, He is Love.
> ~ We are confused, He is Order.
> ~ We are hurting, He is Peace.

And He promised if we SEEK Him, we shall surely find Him.

Eve

Sweet juice ran down Eve's dimpled chin and burnished the skin of the Serpent in the morning sun. The first blood ever seen dripped from the animal skins when God Himself sacrificed them to cover the shame of Adam and Eve. No flimsy leaves would suffice even as temporary atonement.

In His merciful goodness God drove them from the garden paradise, posted Angels with flaming swords like ice so they could not eat of the Tree of Life and live forever in their fallen state.

God had a plan to reveal His Star of Hope in due time.

Eve of Paradise Garden, the most prestigious address.
Bowered in morning glories, blest with midnight mist,
draped in passion flowers, riotous roses without thorns,
honeysuckled bees, new bird songs every morn.
Lions and lambs gamboled under willow wind,
white tigers strolled with deer 'round river bend.
Fresh from the Creator's hand, beauty full blown,
drawn from Adam's side, loved as his own.

Together talked with God in sunset glory,
Revealing the plan for humanity's story.
Bounteous provision for drink and food,
everything that grew pronounced good,
except, one central tree of all knowledge.

Forbidden, not even to touch the edge?
You knew the sound of wisdom,
but heard another voice,
Listened—pondered—deceived—
made your deadly choice.

Quickly found your husband, eager to share,
suddenly weighted with fear and despair.

You had it all, but wanted more, a legacy
to sisters who succumb to the seducer.
We like to think we would not have fallen,
yet stumble over pride, claiming to keep the law,
audaciously blaming you for all our problems,
sorrier for our circumstances than our sin.

We should weep for you and ourselves, when
seeing what we really are, lonely, confused,
searching restlessly to find all that is best.

Eve, my sister, God was not through with you.
Clothed in lion's blood, moved you due
east of Eden, closed the gate of Paradise,
posted angels with flaming swords like ice,
protecting you from tasting the Tree of Life,
whence would come eternal punishment and strife.

Toiling with your husband, work never done,
loving, birthing, suffering pain and joy as one.
Regret, sorrow, longing, breaking your heart,
where was God now, what was His part?

He was as close as your prayer,
love and great grace waiting there,
for you and me. In repentance, I understand,
by the Lamb's life we are held in His hand.
Mercy unlimited, shadow of the Cross,
Paradise regained, at such great cost!

Genesis 1

Tamar

A camel caravan swayed on the horizon out of the rising sun as Abraham answered God's call. Years later the rope that bound the wood onto Isaac's young back rubbed his shoulders raw-red. Together father and son climbed the rocky path to Mt. Moriah's crown where one future day, God would raise an altar-cross where all mankind could be redeemed.

Squabbling twins, named Esau and Jacob, were born to Issac and Rebekah.

The first came forth red all over like a hairy garment.

But the Lord had said, . . . *the older shall serve the younger.* Genesis 25

Jacob labored long for his Rachel and finally the last two of his twelve sons were born of her, heralding the twelve tribes of Israel. But Benjamin's bloody birth cost the life of Rachel on the road to Bethlehem, the very village to also be the birthplace of the coming Christ Child. Her tomb is still there today, guarded by Israeli soldiers.

Two nations lay in the loins of Esau and his younger brother, Jacob, whom God renamed Israel,

You shall no longer be called Jacob, but Israel. Genesis 32

The human stain seeps like disease from generation to generation. A little-known woman named Tamar found her place in the amazing list which Matthew records of the birth- cords tethering Jesus to Adam.

The Holy Scripture reminds us that

Sin is a disgrace to any people. Proverbs 14

Sin cannot be revenged or removed, only forgiven. Though Tamar was dishonored by Judah, he admits she is right in her claim and she is given the high honor to be an ancestor of Jesus the Messiah.

I, Tamar, am not proud of what I have done,
you must understand . . . not proud of what I have done.
A desperate situation and I was justified.
You ladies alone today have other options—
savings—jobs—an acceptable place in society.
I was an outcast, a foreigner, twice widowed.
My father-in-law, Judah, son of Leah and Jacob,
reluctantly promised his youngest son
to care for me, as Hebrew law provided.
Judah reneged on his word—marriage or care,
would have let his son's memory die with no heir.
I had no other choice.

Drying tears, I painted my eyes with kohl,
my mouth red with berry juice,
plaited ribbons in my hair,
humbling myself to sit near the city gate
with other ladies of the night.
It was degrading, a miserable experience,
I prayed as I waited . . .
Judah came along as if he owned the road.
Smiling shyly at him—he turned—
hesitated but a moment—
came back for me.

Armed with the law of protection,
I demanded his ring before he took me.
Some months later he denied my claim
until I held out the dishonored ring.
Judah crumbled like a clod of dirt on the road.
Somehow out of His infinite goodness
God allowed me to birth twin sons
from the house of Judah, Messiah's branch,
and the rest is His Story.

Genesis 38

Rahab

The blood-red cord unwound as Moses led Israel out of bondage in Egypt, across the Red Sea. They followed the pillar of cloud by day and fire by night, painting the desert sky with vermilion shadows over the lonely darkness.

Joshua led the next generation of the sons of Israel into the Promised Land across the River Jordan, challenging them to
Choose whom they would serve. Joshua 24
He led them to the walls of the ancient city of Jericho to a window where a red cord hung.

Rahab, a scarlet cord binds you to the Cross
seven centuries before the nails
pierced the Carpenter's hands.
You, one of the four women named in His genealogy,
How could this be?

You kept a wayside house on the Jericho wall,
before it fell down, providing favors for all,
the location known far and wide, perhaps
a rosy string latched the door.
Was life so hard, reputation so bloodied,
money so short, pride long lost,
fear for survival, no hope for tomorrow,
How could this be?

Hearing of the Hebrew's God,
how the Red Sea had stood aside,
You were trembling,
for His people were advancing in your land.
Wondering if their God would protect you too?

How could this be?

Before the gate was shut, two enemy spies
hid under drying flax on your roof.
Lying, to protect them, revealed
your tender heart melting in the fiery sun,
How could this be?

Rumors ran rampant 'round the walls,
of Amorite kings' crimson robes,
washed in the blood of battle against Israel's army.
Would they do the same to you?
Pledging a vow of kindness
to the Lord of Heaven and Earth,
pleading safety for the family
gathered beneath your roof,
letting down a scarlet cord, you bid the spies god-speed.
How could this be?

Becoming a woman of faith before the trumpet blast,
lauded in the book of Hebrews for courage to believe.
The royal red line included you by God's power,
who brings all things to be.

Joshua 2

Ruth

War and famine ravaged the land but God did not abandon His people.

Some stayed and others fled only to return, humbled, needy, broken in spirit.

Naomi was one of these as was her faithful daughter-in-law. Little did they know that God would bless them with unusual privilege. Under a star-struck sky Ruth obediently sought Boaz as her "kinsman redeemer." God assuaged the bitterness of Naomi's grandmother heart and laid a baby boy on her breast to be the progenitor of the Messiah . . . every Jewish mother's dream of joy to mother such a son! But the mother, Ruth, was a foreigner, a Moabite, a Gentile.

Was there to be room at the Cross for a foreigner, a Moabite, a Gentile, to kneel in repentance? Ruth would declare it is so, for she became the grandmother of King David because of her marriage to Boaz in the Divine red line of Judah, son of Jacob whom God named Israel.

Dear Ruth,
you are often quoted
at weddings and anniversaries
of the heart, I've noted.

Whither thou goest, I will go.
Where thou lodgest, I will lodge.
Thy people shall be my people,
thy God, my God.

A pledge given freely
from your young spirit,
spoken not to husband, already dead,

but to a grief-stricken mother-in law—
like wheat struck flat by hard rain—
in spite of what she said.

You were irresistibly drawn to her
homeland, not knowing where it led,
trusting in the God above all gods,
following in a path you could not see
through tear washed eyes,
but obediently.

Instructed in the widow's way,
permission to glean harvested fields,
gathering grain left behind.
Meeting the kindly master, provider,
protected at his feet until due time
when he proclaimed his love for you.

Respecting the ancient tradition,
to witnesses—he drew off his shoe,
and became your kinsman redeemer,
a picture of what Messiah would do.

Boaz claimed you for his very own,
blessed to be his wife and mother of his son.
He loved you and your love in turn
produced a memorable genealogy.

Your heart joyfully burned to be
grandmother of David, Israel's King;
progenitor of the Messiah, whose
praises the whole world will sing!

Ruth

David's Mother

The Promised Land was settled with the next generations of the sons of Israel. Fire flamed red-hot under the altars of sacrifice and
> Every man did what was right in his own sight. Judges 21

Years of struggle continued under Judges and Prophets until finally the people had their own demand of a King like everyone else, but it was not God's plan of a Theocracy. However, in His infinite love reaching down to His creation, He continued to work through ordinary people like David's mother.

He must have loved you very much.
David, the youngest child of you and Jesse.
The last of eight sons at home in Bethlehem,
still tending his father's flocks in the shepherd's fields,
a millennium before the Angels sang of Peace.

He had your beautiful eyes
and his father's red hair.
Or was it round-about like the sun and moon
that rose and set on his strong shoulders?
Did you teach him to play the harp,
gently fingering the strings,
grace notes and good stories of God's faithfulness
woven together like your finest cloth?

Then tracing the frame with his young fingers
showing the shape of the Kinnereth Sea
that sang far to the north
feeding your river with life-giving water.
Did you cut out the slingshot

from a scrap of leather, so he could
dance stones on the skipping stream?

Certainly your knees were prayer-worn
as he became warrior, king, lover,
sinner, saint, poet, musican.
He never forgot your tender care.
When King Saul's murderous revenge drove
all of you to the cave of Adullam,
David arranged safe-keeping with the
King of Moab, for you and Jesse,
protecting the root of Messiah's branch.

Yes, your son must have loved you very much,
not to leave you alone in that one verse of Scripture.

I Samuel 22

David

King Saul was followed by King David to whom we owe the patterns of praise and petitions in the Psalms. Such eloquence is not easily earned, but forged from the pain and joy of fire and faith. David is so real to us for he has flung our questions to the star-strung heavens as he suffered sin and its consequences on the long climb to the mountaintop from the valley *of the shadow of death.* Psalm 23.

David, how would I dare to write of you . . .
you, the Poet Laureate of all time?
My most mellifluous metaphor is jangling jargon
beside your *green pastures and still waters,*
my sharpest simile but a bubble before your sword
to slay the wicked.

My most honest attempt at confession, pitiful
compared to the baring of your heart's
shameful deed that haunts day and night.

My major hymn of praise like infant babbling beside
You, O Lord are robed with honor, majesty and light.

You teach me the joy of language,
the privilege of passion, the treasure of tears;
you show me the Messiah.
Some readers may prefer the persuasion of Paul,
others the authority of Peter or the insight of John.
But if the only pages of Scripture I had were just
these few thin, underlined, thumbed, worn,
tearstained Psalms, it would be enough . . . .

to be like *a tree planted by the river of water,*
to know that *night after night showeth knowledge,*
to sit where *You prepare a table before me,*
to dwell in Your presence every day of my life.

Create a clean heart in me,
to live under *the shadow of the Almighty,*
I love your law.

I want to *enter Your gates with thanksgiving.*
Bless the Lord O my soul and all that is within me,
You chart the path ahead of me.

David, because of you I *pray for the peace of Jerusalem.*

Let everything alive give praise to the Lord,
Hallelujah!

The Psalms

Bathsheba

But all was not peaceful either in the shepherds' fields of Bethlehem or in the palatial palace of the King in Jerusalem. Bathsheba was commandeered by David to come to him. Together they suffered the pain of the death of their baby for God does not condone sin. Yet, God had promised that His own Son, The Messiah, would come in the flesh through the lineage of David. The Almighty determined that Bathsheba would have the privilege to mother Solomon and thereby appear in the royal red line of the genealogy of Jesus Christ.

He opened His arms wide for all kinds of people: man or woman, free or slave, Jew or Gentile, when He hung on that cruel Cross. The Blood of Salvation poured from His sinless body to atone for the sins of all repentant people since time began.

Bathsheba, I've hesitated to write of you,
difficult to conjecture your world view,
knowing very little of your side
of the story.

I wonder if pride
secreted you, grief robed,
hidden from prying view.
Bearing sorrow in your crown,
avoiding eyes and tongues of town,
you reigned as David's Queen,
with a purpose yet unseen.
As difficult as being a military wife,
lonely in long periods of strife.

That night, were you seducer or victim?

Bathing in sight of him,
the King who stayed home from battle,
his men fighting bravely, death's rattle.
Orders to have your husband killed,
claiming you so rumors stilled
of a child soon to be born.

But God did not condone
transgression with happiness,
taking the infant to Himself.
You were suffering, crying for help,
repentant, as all forgiven sinners are,
knowing well, God will bar
the one so foolish as to say,
sin is not his way.

I think you were truly contrite too,
for Solomon was born of you.
Blessed of God with unusual wisdom,
you had the privilege of mothering him,
raising a King for David's throne,
promised as Messiah's own.

Bathsheba, you were more than movies tell,
knowing pain and blessing, as all women will,
finding life a path through thorns.
Loved by God before you were born.

II Samuel 11

TRUST...

is defined as a positive belief in the honesty, justice and power of a person, or a confident expectation of hope because of that person. These are attributes of the God of the Bible and are clearly presented in the pages of Scripture.

Whom can we trust enough to lead us to the TRUSTworthy one?

Jesus said.
> *You are trusting in God, now trust in Me . . .*
> *I am the Way and the Truth and the Life.*
> *No one can get to the Father except by means of me.*
> John 14

HAVE YOU SEEN THE STAR?

Dr. Luke

How are we to find Him today?
The ancient Scriptures still speak with authority—
alive with eyewitness reports—
news flashes—
Angels—
Christmas carols,
school pagents—
billboards—proclaiming

"Jesus is the Reason for the Season."

*D*ear Dr. Luke,
Physican, Caregiver, Historian, Author,
I am deeply indebted to you.

You searched and researched the truth
with meticulous care;
a surgeon's scalpel dividing history and heresy,
an incision to remove legend from fact,
a stiching together of the Word made flesh—
healing for a wounded world.

Without you, who would know?
Glorious Gabriel's missions
foretelling John the Baptist's birth,
and his Divine cousin to be named Jesus,
the intimate conversations of Elizabeth and Mary,
filled with Holy wonder of God's hand.

Without you, who would know ?
Zacharias' Benedictus,
Mary's Magnificate,
Simeon's song,
Anna's answered prayers.

Without you, who would know?
Angel's bending low
fanning the Shepherd's meager wood to flame,
unrolling Heaven's scroll
with the brilliance of His Name,
spelled in stars on the blackboard sky.
Thank you, Dear Dr. Luke.

Luke

Zacharias

Zacharias had a hard time learning to TRUST even after he spoke with an Angel, but he learned a lesson in his silence to pass on to us. Zacharias had all of the tradition and ritual of his religion in his mind. He was a righteous man serving as a Priest in the temple when the Angel appeared to him. During his enforced silence he came to know God in a much more personal way. After dinner, out under the stars Zacharias finally understood when he studied the vast heavens that religion is not the same as relationship with the Living God.

TRUST

Zacharias, you godly old fool!
Had you labored in the priestly course of Abijah
like the moon shadowing the sun—
so long you could not comprehend Gabriel's meaning?
Burned your fingers on the live coals from the Altar,
when lighting the evening incense,
no longer igniting prayer heavenward
for your beloved, barren Elizabeth.
Old eyes widened, blinking at the brilliance,
a shielding hand across the tired brow, light
penetrating clutched fingers, shoulders shaking
at the soft thunder of His Voice—

Fear not, Zacharias, your prayer is heard.

A rumbling in ears almost closed by time,

*Son—John—joy -
Holy Spirit—Israel - Elijah—*

Delusions of angels, wings whipping wind,
fanning flames, questioning disbelief,
excuses of rational, holy fragrance,
falling to your knees before the
Cloud of Unknowing.

Shadows leaned against the walls
and still you did not come—you godly old fool
struck dumb for disbelief, nine moons to ponder
does God still speak?

Elizabeth, blooming with righteous pride,
had all the last words until you firmly wrote,
that day of celebration - the eighth day of your joy—

His name is John.

Luke 1

Elizabeth

Zacharias' patient wife Elizabeth had quiet time every morning to ponder the meaning of the miracle in her swelling body. In the afternoons, weary and wondering, she knew that the Messiah had not yet been born even though the promise had been given so long ago. In the long dark nights she longed to ask her husband what he was thinking. Perhaps she knotted a red cord to count the days until her delivery. Then her cousin Mary came unexpectedly with amazing news and Elizabeth learned to TRUST God's miracles.

Elizabeth, I wonder what the neighbors said
when Zacharias, struck dumb in awe,
tarried long by the Temple veil
for the vision that he saw?
Priestly duties fulfilled,
he hurried home to you.
A message so wonderful,
with trembling hands he penned,
of new life to be blessed, but until
that promise had breath to cry,
he could not speak
nor fully explain why.

How could this be,
hope for a baby boy?
Tears tangled on your cheeks
in salty ribbons of joy,
as pressed together, kneeling
you worshiped the Lord.
Marveling at His mercy,
wondering at Gabriel's word

of a son of prophecy,
to prepare for the Messiah,
long awaited, as your barrenness,
even the voice of Elijah.
You conceived, as Sarah
did of old, remembering when
the Angel of the Lord
had spoken of God's plan.

As time wove the tapestry of promise
you shared a holy silence,
until your cousin, Mary, came
in miraculous fullness of Spirit.
In hallowed conversation
you knew a sweet communion
of the mysteries of God, and man
needing salvation, for eternal union.

The baby's cry pierced the night,
still your husband could not speak.
The eighth day, for covenanted circumcision,
neighbors came rejoicing, to meet
the son of his name.
You declared it was John,
What manner of child is this?
The father agreed, as one,
immediately he could praise again.

With godly wisdom, in quiet confidence
you raised a passionate son
crying for the world to repent.
Until suddenly, his voice was stilled,
a golden thread, harshly broken,
and the Master Weaver said,
The finest prophet born of woman,
is dead.

Luke 1

The Angel Gabriel

In amazement, Mary and Elizabeth spoke of Angels and answers, prayers and praises. The glorious Gabriel had not only visited Zacharias, but Mary! She had spoken with him in person, like she knew him. She saw him and knew he was God's messenger of good news. Even Joseph, her betrothed, had told of his encounter with the Angel. It was all too wonderful to comprehend completely but they had learned to TRUST God.

Gabriel, of those who long to look at human things,
received the nod of God to spread your wings,
transcending a scarlet sky
spread with clouds, stars, rainbows
arching o'er the storm-spiraled earth below.

Wise men considered your streaking strobe—
flashing fire circling a tottering globe.

You had traced this luminous path but six moons ago.
Neighbors speculated on Elizabeth's maternal glow,
some strange miracle like Sarah of old, could it be so?

Does God above really care for earth,
promising man salvation and eternal worth?

Veering slightly north to Nazareth as dawn broke,
suddenly stood before the maid, Mary, and spoke.

Fear not, for in this Day-star hour
you will know Holy Spirit power.
God's only Divine Son will be born Immanuel.
We will return with glorious news to tell.

Nine times the monthly shofar was blown.
Messiah prepared to leave His heavenly throne,
for the Cradle and the Cross that was His alone.

The Angelic Host unrolled the midnight sky
like Isaiah's scroll.
The bells of the universe began to toll
Holy, Holy, Holy.

Luke 1

Annunciation Day

Mary's TRUST was almost immediate, for she accepted God's will for her after just one question, *How can this be?* Joseph, her fiancé, had a strong struggle with reason, as most of us do when God is at work and we cannot see what He is doing. Joseph hammered heaven with his questions but he could not see beyond the curtain of stars.

The sun struck the darkness like a Roman sword.
I, Joseph, stood offering my praise to the One
who brought light; O not light
just to begin labor, light in my soul—
the Prophet's words echoed
like a hammer striking nails,

*The people who walk in darkness
will see a great light.*

I, Mary, knelt in awe of the startling sunrise,
a piercing shaft, striking north to south
a bar of cloud hung east to west.
Would my bridegroom come today?
Hope rose in my breast like Mt. Tabor
rising out of the valley mist . . .

I was smoothing the new ox yoke,
to be delivered before dusk—

Hurrying to the well, I was strangely alone,
early or late, I did not know, but
I was not alone—a luminous presence—
all the stars of heaven caught in his cloak—

TRUST

silvered words poured over me—

Fear Not!

She came running, stumbling,
grasses clutching her skirt,
breathless words
struck me like mortal blows—

My beloved, Joseph, I have wounded you—

Thunder heads charged,
arrows of rain tore my beard—
falling to my knees,
hammering heaven with questions—
why, God, why?

Dearest, soft words—
cutting as your sharp ax—
strike me too ... my love for you is as pure and sweet
as the snows of Mt. Hermon—

God, I trusted You, wanted to please You—
even serve You in some small way—
polishing the plow handles an extra time,
not to scar the buyer's hands—
O God, why me?
What about her—my love—my joy?
We have been circumspect, honorable,
patient against all desire.
God, I do not understand!
Can I hide her—protect her—send her away?
My God, what did she mean about the Holy Spirit?

If you had only heard the Angel's words, maybe then
you could understand why I responded—

I am the handmaid of the Lord:
let it be to me according to your word.

Darkness crashed like Jericho's wall.
Twisting on my mat restless as wind,
chasing sleep to still the hammer—
the Angel's sword sliced the sound—He spoke—
words of molten silver searing my soul—

Joseph, son of David, do not fear—

I could not know that one day
that scoundrel Matthew, that tax collector,
would tell you what was said—

Matthew 1

ABIDE...

is an old-fashioned word for someone to wait, stay and remain with you, to live with, to endure. Just exactly what everyone is looking for in a friend.

The stars ABIDE in the heavens without any effort at all. They dwell—rest—in that deep bed of blue exactly where God placed them. They do not wander away and reluctantly return but move through their orbits precisely as they were designed to do.

We build planetariums to study the heavens, we exclaim over the beauty of the stars, we send astronauts to the moon and beyond to learn about our origins.

Jesus said,
> ABIDE with me and let my Word ABIDE in you.
>   John 15

Certainly, this is the most wonderful invitation ever given to men and women and children.

The Innkeeper

The night fell like a blanket on the hills and valleys of Israel, a black blanket tucked into every curve and cave where Isaiah had promised 700 years before that

The people that sit in darkness will see a great light.

For a child is born to us, a Son will be given to us, and the government shall rest upon His shoulders and His name will be called Wonderful, Counselor, Mighty God, Eternal Father, Prince of Peace.

Isaiah 9

Mary and Joseph had the Word in their hearts when they arrived at the Inn in Bethlehem needing a place to rest. They were in the precise place that the Father had ordained when He spoke to Micah the prophet centuries before . . . Bethlehem in Judah.

We call you old in the Christmas pageants, perhaps
you were merely a young son, sent to unbolt the door.
We malign you as mean-spirited and cutting
as a sharp wind on a lonely night.
We accuse you of our locked hearts, there is
no room at the Inn of the Soul.

Frantic with preparation of food, frustrated
with stacks of gifts to buy, bills to pay,
overwhelmed with cards to write, aggravating
burned out lights, exhausting parties and pageants—
are the angel wings on straight—careful
the shepherd doesn't trip on his robe!

One snow-bright Christmas Eve,

Great-grandfather Kennedy
taught me the lesson of the Innkeeper.
I poured more steaming coffee as we gathered
around the glowing Tree. Daddy added fragrant
pine to the fire, as the Grandmother-Angels,
softly singing Silent Night,
fluttered their imaginary wings.
Grandpa A.E., governor of Syria, ordered the census.
Our young son, as Joseph, readied the donkey-dog,
big sister cradled her baby doll and walked wearily
to the Inn of the Living Room.

The compassion in the Innkeeper's eyes,
the caring in his outstretched hands,
the tenderness in his voice—
No room at the Inn,
but come with me to the stable,
the animal's steam will warm you,
the hay is dry and sweet, there will be no charge.
You are my guests in this poor humble abode.

Luke 2

Bethlehem Shepherds
Circa 5 B.C.

Angels proclaimed Joy to the World. Their glowing wings fanned the weak fire to red flame. The Hallelujah Chorus polished the dome of heaven with celestial music. And the morning stars heralded the birth of the King of Kings and Lord of Lords.

Nearby in the Shepherds' fields the cold light of a meager fire burned fitfully as they blew on their raw, red hands. The sheep were asleep, all accounted for, any cuts oiled against infection; safe. The icy stars were close enough to touch when a singular STAR appeared on the black horizon like a flaming torch held high. It blazed beauty, burning the night for fuel, moving inexorably toward their hillside . . .

Congratulations Graduates!
First to receive honors from the Bethlehem Bible College,
David's rough fields your classrooms 21 centuries
before today's golden stone walls; eons
before your school opened the public library . . .

By day, practice in animal husbandry,
by night, lessons of the wonder of the Gospel
written in the stars. The silent mystery
of the sheepfold for the sons of Abraham
spoken of in star names as old as time:
The Redeemer, The Bruised One, The Branch.
Names glowing like embers in the evening fires:
Arcturus, Orion, Pleiades.

The cycle of the seasons well known to you
as the bleating of spring lambs searching

summer's green pastures.
Light followed darkness, stillness shadowed the wind,
rain burst from welcome clouds.
The sun gave warmth, the moon rolled it away
and star-ships sailed in the deep sea of heaven
as recorded by Job, the Patriarch.
But nothing prepared you for the celestial chorus.

Suspended brilliance, awesome, over-arching presence,
fearful beauty, glorious thunder, they spoke as one,

Fear Not!

A valedictory hymn of praise pouring like oil
on your heads and beards—good news,
joy, peace for the whole world.

Gathering up ragged robes you ran to find the Saviour.
We tell the story still and long for His Peace.

Yesterday, in a Christmas market in a land far away,
I met a man from Bethlehem,
inquired if the Bible College withstood recent battles.
His eyes lit with Shepherd's fire,
You know of our school?

I have visited and contributed books to your library.

Well I am a graduate of Bethlehem Bible College!
I go to tell the world that Light
still dispels darkness.

Luke 2

King Herod

The astonished men gathered their robes close and ran like the wind headlong into the sleeping village, straight to the stable to fall on their knees before the miraculous sight. A baby born in David's town, to be ...*good news to all men of peace*... except King Herod.

The King's fury burned in his breast like a roaring fire, anger that this babe should be born in his jurisdiction—-fear of an uprising of shepherds and common men—- jealousy for his throne. He stood on the vast porches of the Antonio Fortress, shaking his fists at the winking stars. He congratulated himself on his subterfuge with the visitors from the East. He would find that baby and destroy him!

Herod, who named you Great?
Certainly it fit your ego, with a golden crown
flashing in the desert sun.
Friend of Tiberius Caesar, ingratiating favor,
building that playground in the north,
Tiberius on the Sea.
A jewel worthy of an Emperor—
a sapphire ringed by emerald hills of Galilee,
heedless that it rested on a graveyard.
Unclean for any Jew, a resort fit for Romans.

Herod, who named you Great?
Caesarea, another namesake jewel,
a necklace of light around the throat
of a deep harbor, carefully dredged to provide
safe shelter from the sometimes jealous Sea.
An ingenious double wall to keep out undesirables,

a magnificent amphitheater for amusements played
on a vast stage with the Mediterranean
a turquoise curtain.

Herod, you knew how to live well—like a King—
but for those troublesome Jews,
always a pain in your pleasure.
Much could be gained by letting them
rebuild Solomon's Temple.
Let them worship their invisible god
and offer smelly sacrifices.
You ordered your finest engineers
to level Mt. Moriah's crown,
where Abraham's raised hand was stayed by an Angel.
Laborers leveraged huge stones
to build a supporting wall
to the west, ordered servant stonemasons to hew the
back-breaking building-blocks—46 years to complete.

Herod the Great, your crowning achievement—
a popularity ploy.
Consuming jealousy feeds on such an ego,
rumors ravaged dreams, a King to be born of the Jews?
An extraordinary daystar heralded his birth,
but where could He be found?
No time now for a play in Caesarea,
cancel the weekend in Tiberius,
pretend to seek him for homage,
solicit the traveling astrologers,
summon the swordsmen of the Antonia Fortress
to deal with this threat.
Slaughter the babies of Bethlehem!

Herod the Great, from your grave do you still hear,
Rachel weeping for her children?

Matthew 2

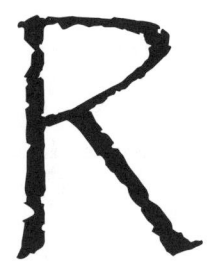

REJOICE...

To REJOICE implies that the individual is so full of God's joy that his life overflows in thanksgiving and thanks-*living*.

God has His men and women all over the world in every age, those who have learned to REJOICE in all circumstances because they know His matchless love for them.

Jeremiah, the prophet, has words of testimony for people today . . .

> *Your words became for me a joy and the delight of my heart.*
>
> Jeremiah 15

The Wise Men

The rich caravan from the East slowed on the hillside before Jerusalem. The wise men carried treasure boxes of precious gifts wrapped with strong cords the color of sunrise. They marveled at the golden sight of the Glorious Temple rising above the walls of the city. Surely this must be the Temple of a great King.

They would pay their respects and press on until the miraculous STAR they were following finally stopped. They rejoiced and sang Psalms of ascent,

> *Our feet are standing within your gates*
> *O Jerusalem.*
>
> Psalm 122

sensing that their journey to find the King of the Jews was almost completed.

How did you know it was His star?
Did you have ancient prophets' scrolls to study?
Were you perhaps Jews,
descendants of Queen Esther's people,
those who sat weeping and hung their harps
in the willow trees?
Did they stay behind when Ezra and Nehemiah
led the return to Jerusalem?
After the first Purim celebration
was business very good in Babylon?

Did you debate what Isaiah meant when he wrote that
A Virgin shall bear a Son,
and ponder how to find Bethlehem in Judea
where Micah had spoken of the birthplace?

Did you nightly search the black-tented desert skies for
The Star that would arise out of Jacob?

There was no more wondering.
Suddenly out of the pit of night, radiance rose,
brilliance beyond measure. Without mistake,
this was a supernatural star, indeed,
The Daystar.

Friends called you foolish.
Hastily packing for an arduous journey,
preparing gifts for an Infant King,
a mission without precedent.

The Star moved, you followed with courage like Daniel.
Dry days, lavish nights under the Star-struck sky
until Jerusalem appeared like a golden city
descending out of heaven
and The Star stood still over a stable.

Yes, Isaiah, Micah, your directions were accurate.
A Star did rise out of Jacob, from the house of David.
Wise men still kneel before the
King of Kings.

Matthew 2

Simeon

Simeon, a quiet devout man, knew God through the ancient Scriptures. He found reason to REJOICE in quoting the Word as he walked to and from the Temple, fingering the knots on his prayer shawl—*the tallit*—each knot recalling a particular law. He understood David saying he loved the law of God. Simeon waited, believing the prophecies of the coming Messiah.

𝒢od's good morning, faithful Anna,
His blessing be upon you.
Did the stone-cold seep into your bones?
Surely spring warmth is due,
winter's dark is long and deep
but ewes are offering with plaintive bleat,
Shepherds tend fields, lamb-sweet.

My soul exalts our Creator.
Today dawned with promise bright,
His promised hope is David's Son,
did you see the Daystar at edge of night?
One day the Prophet's words will be
fulfilled, all Israel will see
Jacob's star arise to set us free.

My soul was strangely lightened
but seven days ago
as if my spirit were lifted
above darkened earth below!

Look, the Infant!

I see God's Salvation
for Jew and Gentile of every nation!
Anna, now I depart with exultation!

Luke 2

Anna

And then there are those who know God through Prayer; whose every breath is full of praise. REJOICING is the language of their heart. Anna was such a woman. She is known only as a praying woman, but that must be the finest praise to be said of any woman. She appears briefly in Scripture after a lifetime of prayer.

Anna, of the happy tribe of Ashur,
your profession was prayer.
At the temple day and night,
what was the secret
that kept you there?

I, too, love to pray,
but it is not my food and drink,
not my every breath.
A whisper of confession,
a pleading petition,
forgetting too often, to praise
the Maker of all my days.

Paul said to pray without ceasing,
he must have known about you.
Married only seven years
before your husband died.
Certainly, you must have cried
before the Lord, asking why?

Or was it sufficient to know
that He cared.
Did you not complain of aches and pain?

Or just listen to hear your name,
hushing the host of heaven,
Anna is praying of again.

I understand, confession clears
the way to the throne of God.
Praise then, for who He is,
not just for what He has done.
Thanksgiving, never ceasing,
opens the door to petition.

Just to be in His presence
is time sweetly spent,
as in the words of the Psalmist,

*One thing have I asked
of God, that will I seek,
that I may dwell in Your presence,
Every day of my life, delighting
in your incomparable perfection and glory.*

When they brought the infant, Jesus,
you prophesied this very one to be
the redemption of Israel
for which you had long prayed.

Anna, I would learn of thee,
faithfulness for what I cannot see.

Luke 2

Bethlehem was the center of the world that incredible day over 2000 years ago, the Birthday of the King of Kings. Now we push the edges of space but we cannot make peace in that small village; pools of red blood seep into the thirsty land. All of our efforts seem futile.

The world waits for the Messiah to come . . . the Prince of Peace.

>But as for you Bethlehem, from you One will go forth to be a ruler in Israel. His goings forth are from long ago, from the days of Eternity.

Micah 5

Bethlehem Song

O little town of Bethlehem
how still we see thee lie

Slingshots sing a sorry hymn o'er Bethlehem's fields,
sheep shudder at the mournful whine of mortar music.
Souvenir shops stand empty with hosts of silent angels,
Nativity Church in Manger Square looms in loneliness.
The Eye of the Needle is closed to worshipers,
and Rachel's Tomb is soldiered against prayer.

Above thy deep and dreamless streets
the silent stars go by

An aching sun will rise o'er rubbled streets,
anxious women hurrying early to the well.
The men labor repairing ravage from the night,
and children gather rocks before the school bell.
Shepherds calm frightened flocks in their fields
while sandbags are stacked against blue doors.

Yet in thy dark streets shineth
the everlasting Light

Candles of conciliation sputter hopefully,
healers of hurts work long and feverishly,
the faithful gather quietly in dark homes to pray.
Warm bread is baking in Bethlehem—
the house of bread—
and we long for the coming of the Prince of Peace.

The hopes and fears of all the years
are met in thee tonight.

REFLECTION

Seek
Trust
Abide
Rejoice

    Bethlehem seems very far away indeed, yet as close as CNN. So where are you on your Christmas journey this year? All wrapped, packed and singing *Joy to The World*, or somewhere not quite as far down the road as you would like to be?

    This joyous season is often the most miserable season for many. The mistletoe and holly are missing. The red ribbons lie tangled in the drawer. You could not be more frightened than—

    Tamar was for her future alone,
Rahab, facing enemy occupation in her city,
Ruth was a foreigner herself with few options,
David's Mother had to flee for her life in wartime,
Bathsheba had to cope with the death of her child,
David knew he had sinned against God.

    All of them found their answers as they learned what it meant to SEEK God.

    As Eve found out,

    Where was God now, what was His part?

He was as close as your prayer,
love and great grace waiting there,
for you and me, in repentance I understand,
by the Lamb's life we are held in His hand.
Mercy unlimited, shadow of the Cross,
Paradise regained, at such great cost.

Zacharias and Elizabeth, Joseph and Mary, two couples who had their own lives turned upside down when touched by an angel, and God-side up again when they learned to TRUST the One who loved them.

As Paul reminds us, *No one who believes in Him will ever be disappointed.*
Romans 10

Even ordinary people, especially ordinary people like Innkeepers, Shepherds, and Kings need to know where there is a safe place to live in this terror-taunted world. It has been said by a modern-day wise-man that the safest place in the world is to be in the center of God's will.

As I learn to ABIDE in His Word, I find,

. . . there I'll be when trouble comes, He will set me high on a rock out of reach of all my enemies.
Psalm 27

The Wise Men, Simeon and faithful, praying Anna, all lived under the watchful authority of the Roman occupation. Yet, they each found reason to REJOICE in JESUS, the BRIGHT AND MORNING STAR.

I pray that you, too, will see the STAR.

~Joyce Carr Stedelbauer